THE THIEF

THERE IS A THIEF THAT COMES IN THE NIGHT.
HE CLEVERLY HIDES FAR OUT OF SIGHT.
HE COMES STEALING UP THE STAIR AND NOT ADP OR ATT OR ANYTHING YOU DO OR SAY CAN KEEP THIS BRAIN THIEF AWAY.

YOU CAN INSTALL SECURITY DEVICES BUT THE BRAIN SPLICES WILL CONTINUE WITHIN YOU.
YOUR REALITY IS NO LONGER REALITY.

EACH DAY YOU AWAKEN IN A NEW DAY AND IN A WAY YOU CANNOT UNDERSTAND BECAUSE EACH DAY IS A NEW LAND AND YOU CAN'T FIGURE OUT WHERE YESTERDAY WENT TO.. NOW YOU'VE BEEN SENT TO A NEW VENUE WHERE NOTHING MAKES SENSE HENCE
 THEY CALL IT CONFUSION BUT TO YOU IT'S A DELUSION
WITH THESE PEOPLE CALLING YOU MOM OR DAD BUT THE LIFE YOU HAD IS FORGOTTEN AND NOW YOU'RE JUST WANTING TO KNOW WHO YOU ARE...AND WHY YOU ARE HERE AND YOU CAN'T REMEMBER THE DAY, THE MONTH OR THE YEAR...

AFTER WHILE IT DOESN'T MATTER
BECAUSE THE LAUGHTER IS GONE
SO YOU TRY TO GET ALONG WHILE
THIS THIEF WHO CANNOT BE
ARRESTED WHO HAS NESTED IN
YOUR TANGLED BRAIN.. WHO HAS
MADE YOU NO LONGER SANE..
ALZHEIMER'S DEMENTIA HAS
GAINED A VICTIM ...YET AGAIN.

BY LORI TROTTER, RN
3/2418

FORWARD

Hi. My name is Lori Trotter. I have been an RN in the state of Texas for 40 years. Mostly I have worked with the elderly but I began my career as an RN in pediatrics. When I switched to caring for the elderly people told me..."Oh! You will never laugh again!"

How wrong they were. I love caring for the elderly. I have learned much from our nation's seniors. They have given me so much more than I feel I have given them.

If you are reading this book you have a loved one who has been diagnosed with this disease that has been termed "The Great Thief". It is always hard to watch a loved one reach the end life.

This particular disease I think makes it harder. I hope this book helps you in your journey. You about to enter some Murky Water.

NAVIGATING MURKY WATER, A CAREGIVER'S GUIDE TO DEMENTIA

By Lori Trotter, RN

Cover Credit: Lori Trotter, RN

DEDICATION

This book is dedicated to the many patients who suffer from this disease, and their families and the nurses who work tirelessly to assist in their comfort and care.   And most of all to our dear friends "Jerry" and "Ginny" whose names have been changed but whom we hold dearly in our hearts.

CHAPTER ONE
THE DIAGNOSIS

Jerry was 56 years old on his way to work one day and suddenly realized he didn't recognize his surroundings. At first he thought he might have just been day dreaming and missed his exit. He looked around and saw nothing familiar. He decided to pull over to the side of the road and to set his GPS so he could find his way and then the truth hit him....he didn't know his destination.

He sat there for a minute and tried to focus. Finally he called his girlfriend, Ginny, and told her he was lost. She teased him a bit and said, "How did you manage to do that? You've been driving the same route to work for 10 years!"

"Work! He thought to himself, "I'm going to work!" Something clicked in his brain. He thanked her and began driving again.

Twice more in the next few weeks he had to stop on his way to work and figure out where he was. He began writing down the address to his job and keeping it in his truck.

Then one day, he had to call Ginny again. This time he said,
"Hey do you know what I did with the paper?"

"What paper?" she asked, confused. She had noticed he was beginning to act strangely around the house and she was becoming concerned.

"The paper I write down my work address on," he answered.
"Then, when I get lost, I don't have to call you."

She routed him back home and met him there. They went straight to the doctor. The doctor explained to them that Jerry had early onset dementia. After multiple tests it was determined that he had Alzheimer's disease.

"Alzheimer's!" they both declared in astonishment. They had just about decided that Jerry had had a stroke and was suffering memory loss from brain damage caused by a clogged artery in his brain. Except that unlike stroke damage, which usually stabilizes or gets better, Jerry's memory was getting worse. Ginny noted that he had forgotten how he liked his coffee and what side of the bed he slept on. She had mentioned the problem to his brother who had expressed concern. Now this? Alzheimer's! Jerry was only 56 years old!

Of course we all have memory lapses. Just as Jerry originally thought that he had been day-dreaming and missed his exit that first day, we all get lost from time to time. How many times have you stepped into a room and forgotten your purpose for going in there?

In our busy, multi-tasking lives we frequently lose our car keys, cell phones, pens, paper, purses, wallets. There are even devices now that we can attach to frequently misplaced objects so we can find them more easily. You meet someone at a party and six months later you cannot remember his name. There has been a whole lot of events going on in your life in the last six months and his name got crowded out.

Sometimes you may have forgotten what you had for breakfast...or even if you had breakfast. Neurologists say this is normal behavior. Our brains occasionally may skip around a bit.

However, there are other, stronger, warnings signs.

Your dad comes out of the bathroom one day with his toothbrush in his hand and says, "What's this for?" Your mom calls you and says, "I'm worried about Dad. I think we should take him the doctor. He couldn't remember Fluffy's name today. We have had that cat for 5 years. "

I once knew a professional lady who was an ombudsman for the elderly. She was very intelligent and very involved in her community. She showed up a meeting with a very odd purple hat. Mostly people laughed it off as a sign of her sense of humor or maybe as a sign of reference to a poem by Sandra Halderman Martz, "When I Am I Shall Wear Purple". Then one wintry day she slipped off her overcoat to reveal she had come to the assembly wearing nothing but her underwear.

People with early onset may forget to take their pills that morning. Many people do that. But people who forget they have pills to take or what they are for may need further testing.

Generally, if memory loss is interfering with one's ability to care for one's self, his job or his family relationships, it may be time to take notice.

People with Alzheimer's eventually cannot care for themselves. They cannot use a stove because they forget how it works or may cause a fire. Sometimes they forget they must stay at home and attempt to drive their car or someone else's car. They forget about safety issues and may walk out into traffic. As the disease progresses they are unable to attend to their hygiene. They forget to take a shower or even how to operate the bathtub. Eventually they will lose control of their body wastes and will need to wear protective clothing. They may not know family members or friends, even close care takers. They need constant supervision.

CHAPTER TWO
What to Expect

There are many stages of Alzheimer's dementia and as much as people may vary they all go through pretty much the same ones.

These are seven of the most common according to Web MD:

Alzheimer's Stage 1

In stage 1 of Alzheimer's, a patient will show no symptoms of the disease. While it may not seem logical to include this stage, since the disease has yet to affect cognition, medical professionals include it because the disease is technically present in the patient at this point, even if it's not yet noticeable.

Alzheimer's Stage 2

In stage 2, the cognitive decline associated with the disease begins to appear, but only in very mild ways. At this point, many patients assume their memory troubles are simply due to getting older, since they revolve around things like misplacing keys or trouble recalling names of acquaintances— both of which are common memory lapses in people aged 65 or older. There are still no symptoms associated with dementia in stage 2.

Alzheimer's Stage 3

By stage 3, the symptoms of Alzheimer's are still fairly subtle, but it is possible for people to be diagnosed with the disease at this point. In addition to forgetting names or misplacing objects, patients in stage 3 may also begin repeating themselves frequently, have difficulty performing tasks at home or on the job, have difficulty with organization, and be unable to develop new skills. By this point, most people associated with the patient will begin to realize that their memory troubles are more than just a symptom of getting older. Stage 3 may last as little as two years or as long as seven.

Alzheimer's Stage 4

Patients in stage 4 can quite accurately be diagnosed as having Alzheimer's disease. Their cognitive decline will start to affect their ability to do everyday tasks at home—such as getting dressed or preparing meals. Additionally, some patients may undergo emotional changes, such as unusual moodiness, due to the confusion that accompanies their decline. Because of these increased difficulties, patients with stage 4 Alzheimer's may not be able to live on their own. The average length of stage 4 is about two years.

Alzheimer's Stage 5

By stage 5, living alone is not a viable option for Alzheimer's patients. As the disease progresses to this point, they will have difficulty recalling memories that should otherwise be easy to remember—their birthday, their address, the current day of the week, or weather conditions.

However, this information is not completely lost. Instead, they may be able to recall it at certain times and under certain conditions but not at others.

Alzheimer's Stage 6

By stage 6, patients lose the ability to perform the most basic of functions, including bathing and using the restroom. Additionally, they may begin to confuse people they see regularly— mistaking a child for a spouse, for example. However, as stage 6 progress, they will begin to forget these people entirely. In terms of personality, stage 6 marks a radical and often distressing shift. Patients typically become more afraid and angrier than in earlier stages, and it becomes increasingly difficult to console them.

Alzheimer's Stage 7

In the final stage, patients must be continually supervised and assisted in order to survive. Speech function gradually diminishes to the point where responses become one or two words at the most. By the end of stage 7, patients are unable to walk, stand, or sit without support, and eventually they even lose the ability to hold their heads up unassisted. The average life span for patients in stage 7 is one and half years, and the most common cause of death is pneumonia.

Although this does not happen to all patients, aberrant, even harmful, behavior may be noticed. I had to have a meeting with a lady one day because her dad was lifting ladies' skirts in the dining room and making crude remarks. She was astounded.

She said, "I used to wonder how my brothers and sisters and I were even conceived. We never saw mom and dad do so much as hold hands. They both acted like touching each other was against the law."

Naomi Feil, who was an Alzheimer researcher, said that people have certain tasks that they must perform during their lives. If they don't feel they have performed these tasks well during the productive parts of their lives they may well try to perform them later. People who were sexually depressed before dementia may become overtly sexual later.

We have seen the same thing with people who were very mild mannered and gentle. Once the dementia progressed, they became angry, physical, and almost violent. Family members may not want to admit these outbursts to everyone and as a matter of fact I once took care of a lady who was caring for her husband with quickly advancing dementia. I had asked her each time I visited them if he was becoming physical. I had noticed how gruffly he spoke to her. Each time she denied it and explained to me that it was the disease causing him to "talk so ugly".

 One day I noticed bruises and she finally broke down and told me that he had been indeed striking her.

 "It's not his fault," she protested.

"Yes," I answered. "I understand that. But his fault or not you are still in danger." It was time to begin the difficult conversation about alternate placement.

Although Alzheimer's usually does not begin until the 60-70 year range many people, like Jerry, may develop it earlier. And like Jerry and Ginny, many may not be aware of it having been in the family.

There are many types of dementia caused by many different types of conditions, such as stroke, mental illness, organic brain disease and sometimes diabetes may cause memory problems. Alzheimer's, however, accounts for 60-70% of the cases of dementia. It is suspected through special testing and also by ruling out other causes. Alzheimer's cannot be definitely diagnosed until after death when brain tissues is examined.

Alzheimer's has been around a long time but it was not until 1906 when Dr. Alois Alzheimer who finally isolated this disease through biopsy. He called it a "peculiar disease" and through the years we still don't know much about it. He discovered that the brain tissue becomes "tangled". We really don't know for sure what makes the brain tissue becomes tangled and although there are some medications which may slow the progression there is no cure. The survival rate from diagnosis appears to be about 3 to 7 years.

There are options, of course. Let's look at a few of them. The three main ones are Assisted Living, Nursing Home, In-Home Care.
Whichever you choose, the going will be rough.

CHAPTER THREE
ASSISTED LIVING FACILITIES

You Get What You Pay For

Assisted Living Facilities vary a great deal in price range, amenities and care. Some are quite lovely and also have a quite lovely price. Assisted Living Facilities, or ALF's, are different from a nursing home, or Long Term Care facility.

An ALF may not have a nurse 24 hours a day, although one may be available on call. When looking at this option, be sure to find out what services are available. Some folks just need a place to live and meals to be served. They may be independent taking their own meds and may even be able to perform such tasks as making their own beds, gathering their clothes for washing, or preparing themselves a meal in the small kitchen available in most of these places. Some even have their own cars and are quite independent in the community.

However, to all things there is a cost so let's just look at some things you may be charged for in addition to your rent. (which usually ranges from $1500 to $2500 a month.

In most ALF's apartment rent includes just that...apartment rent. Housekeeping services, medication distribution, pet care will probably be an extra charge. Usually meal service is included in the basic rent but if the meal has to be carried to a room there is a charge.

Also you may be charged for laundry, bathing and dressing assistance, and transportation to Drs. Appointments.

It's important when you are making this decision to ask a lot of questions and be sure if this is going to be a good fit for your loved one. Remember that as the disease progresses (and it will) the care will increase. As will the charges.

Eventually your loved one may require movement to the Memory Unit. Even if you don't need one right now it's a good idea to check it out on your tour. If you know the facility has a memory unit it may save having to make a change later.

Memory Units are secure units. That is, the doors are locked and they usually require a code for access. They are typically not as fancy as the general living area since the people that live in them require assistance with bathroom needs. The staff to patient ratio is higher as these people require more care. The pricing is very different in this unit, the base pricing being higher but covers more amenities (ie med pass, bathing, etc.) Depending upon the facility, the staff will usually try to involve the patients in activities, walking, etc. When visiting the Memory Unit, look for these things:

1.   How secure is the unit? When entering and exiting does the staff make sure that residents stay inside. Are there any other doors in and out of the unit? Are they also secure?

2.   Frequently there is an outside patio which is fenced and gated. Check the gate. Be sure it is secured.

3.   Who gives the meds? What kind of training do they have? Are they Certified Medication Aides or "off the street people" who have been oriented to the cart? I have worked (and trained) some excellent non licensed personnel

but asking about their orientation and training is always a good idea. Some of the drugs used in the treatment of dementia are pretty powerful. Make sure the person who is passing meds to your mom knows what they are doing!

4.   Ask about night staffing. Is there someone who strictly stays in the unit at night? In some facilities there is someone assigned but due to short staffing the unit is the first place they pull from. The ideal is to have someone there all of the time. If they need to leave for a lunch break someone should come relieve them. Things can happen pretty fast in a Dementia Unit at 3am!

5.   Will they be provided incontinent care throughout the night? This means will someone come check on them, be

sure their protective underwear (diaper) is changed and they are turned and repositioned in the bed if they are unable to do this by themselves. Nasty bed sores and infections can happen if people are allowed to lie in their waste all night.

6.   Look at the patients. Do they look reasonably well groomed? Are they just sitting around staring blankly or are they engaged with staff? What is meal time like? Are they being assisted to eat? Ask the caregivers how they know which patients must have a pureed diet. Choking is common on a dementia unit as the ability to remember to chew and swallow frequently fades.

7.   Ask the staff how they deal with conflicts. Sometimes patients will have some minor conflicts and skirmishes. This is very common as social skills become diminished. How are these handled?

8.   Check for restraints. It is illegal to restrain patients. Even putting a wheelchair locked up against a table that prohibits movement is considered a restraint. People that tend to wander and fall must be carefully monitored. Ask how these challenges are met.

9.   Get to know the staff. These are generally low paying jobs so for some of the workers it may be their second job. Fatigue in workers is a common

problem in all facilities. I have walked into a unit many a time and found workers dozing on the couch. They don't stay asleep long!

10. Look at general cleanliness. Is the area reasonably clean? Bear in mind of course that a dementia unit is like a day care center for very large toddlers. There are likely to be random spills, may be some clutter on the floor occasionally. But how are these things handled? Is the attitude, "Oh, housekeeping will take care of it" or do caregivers take pride in keeping their unit clean.

11. Ask the Administrator if you can come to a Family Council Meeting

before placement or ask if you can visit any of the families. Of course any place has its challenges but knowing about the pitfalls beforehand can really be helpful.

CHAPTER FOUR
LONG TERM CARE FACILITIES
The low down on long term care

The next step is usually a long term care facility (Nursing home). Of course the pricing is different than an Assisted Living Facility but many do accept Medicaid. They also have licensed staff on duty 24 hours a day and many of the amenities that cost extra in an ALF are part of the package in a nursing home. I have worked in long term care for years and I am frequently the "go to" person in choosing one. Here are some of the criteria I go by:

1.   Forget the crystal goblets. Most facilities have only a certain amount of money to take care of each resident. I look around for the "Gingerbread". If there are crystal goblets on the tables and the lobby is filled with mahogany and heavy curtains at the windows chances are the staff isn't paid well. Unless this facility is very upscale and privately paid this rule usually holds well.

2.   If you are taking a tour of the facility request to go off the beaten path. You will be shown the hall on which they are thinking of placing your family member, possibly the physical therapy department and location of the nurse's station and dining room. Ask to see the kitchen.

Of course you will not be allowed to go in there but a kitchen can reveal a lot. Examine the floors. Do you see roaches or roach droppings? Do all of the kitchen help wear hair nets? (A regulation mandated by the state). Is the dirty dish room full of dirty dishes and no one is washing them? Where are the clean plates stacked? Do they look clean. Where is the coffee pot located? Is it in a safe place where on one can burn themselves? Is it clean?

3. Ask how often showers are given. What happens on off shower days? If your family member is incontinent how often will they be changed? State mandate is two hours. If your patient is non

ambulatory, he must also be turned every two hours as well to avoid pressure areas.

4. Find a nurse's aide and ask them how many patients they are caring for today. Ask to see some of their patients. If you notice that the aide proudly shows off your patients, she is someone who truly loves her job. If you are allowed to, walk into someone's room and turn on a call light, see how long it takes to answer the light. State mandate is five minutes.

5. Look at the residents, especially on the hall where you will be placing your loved one. How do they look? Is their

hair clean, clothes reasonably straight? If you are on a dementia hall take into account that it is not always easy to get these people to wear clothes properly...or at all! Still, they should be basically clean looking and well groomed. Fingernails may be a little grimy but they should be properly trimmed.

6. Speak to the residents. Understand that they may not always make sense but if most of them seem to be afraid of you this may be a red flag. Also, residents on a dementia hall who mostly seem to have glazed over eyes and a faraway look may be over medicated.

7.   Dementia hall residents usually have their own activity and dining area. Try to get there at meal time so you can see what is going on. Are the meals being monitored? There should always be staff available. Are people who need help eating being assisted?

8.   Speak to the nurses. To how many people do they pass pills every day? Are the med carts locked when the nurse is not there? Of course they will tell you yes but observe the cart when the nurse walks away.

9.   You can ask to see the results of the last inspection. This is supposed to be displayed on the wall. Ask about anything you don't understand. If the

facilities had deficiencies, which means they did not meet state standards in some area, ask to see the plan of correction. Then ask to see documentation about how that plan is being carried out. The more questions you ask the more comfortable you will be.

10. Look on your loved one's hall for safety issues. Many people with dementia still smoke. How is that done? Are they monitored? Most typically they are taken outside or to a specialized smoking area on a routine basis. What about when the weather is bad? Are the cigarettes and lighters locked away safely? What about aerosols or other types of containers. According to state

mandate these must be locked away on a dementia hall and not available to residents. There should also be a fire extinguisher in the smoking area.

This may seem intrusive but you are putting your momma, who may have forgotten who she is, in with a group of strangers who have forgotten who they are. Ask how many pressure areas (bed sores) the facility currently has. Is there a wound doctor or a treatment nurse who cares for these? How often has the State been called in for complaints. You can ask to see these records. What about if you want to come in after hours? Is there a special code to use? Many homes now have video tape surveillance. Does this home have one?

After you have finally chosen the facility, don't be stranger. Try to visit at odd times, not always the same time and day. It never hurts to bring doughnuts or some special treat in for the staff. Those people work very hard. If you do have a problem, bring it up first with the nurse. Be sure to get a name. "The-nurse-on-moms hall- I- forget- what- day- it- was" is not very helpful when trying to track down a problem. He or she is the one in charge after hours. Of course if you have a valid complaint it can always be brought up the Administrator or Director of Nursing. If you still cannot get your problem resolved there is a number for the ombudsman or health department easily available. It's usually best (and fastest) to try to work things out with the staff first. "Calling the State" is a frequently used threat families use to resolve a problem. Depending upon the severity of the allegation, the State may not come to inspect the incident for days...or even weeks. They actually have a whole year to investigate but it rarely takes that long. If the complaint is invalidated (which it usually is in most places) no changes are made. It's always better to meet the concern at the source.

Routine is very important to dementia patients. Think carefully before you decide to take them home or on a visit out of the facility. Just getting into a car or driving down the road may trigger a negative memory. Occasionally family members decide to take Dad to a funeral. This does not always have a positive ending!

One time a priest came to inform a lady that her brother had passed. She had no children and had had seven siblings. Because she had dementia she did not remember that all of her other siblings were gone. As she asked about each one she was told that they had all died. To her, she had lost her whole family that day. She was depressed for a week. She did not remember what she was depressed about.

Since dementia patients often don't communicate well it may be difficult to understand why they suddenly begin crying, laughing, or yelling. It is usually best if you go visit rather than take them out. More frequent, short visits tend to be better than less frequent, longer ones. The old adage "The squeaky wheel gets the grease" is very true in any kind of elder care. It's usually helpful to visit during a meal time or an activity. This gives you more of an opportunity to interact directly and see for yourself if they need assistance with feeding or can tolerate their food.

Remember the caregivers may have as many as 10 to 15 people to care for and monitor. Your help and input is always appreciated. You might even volunteer to assist with a shower or hair combing. It's amazing how these simple things can help.

Sometimes people with dementia go into paranoid states. They may tell you strange tales such as "They are shooting people in here" or "The police came last night and arrested everyone." Try your best to reassure your family member that everything is calm now and you are there. If you hear repeatedly however, "Someone beat me up last night", and you see evidence of this, pay attention. Probably it is dementia rambling but may not always be. Look for bruises or reddened areas. Ask questions. Investigate. Nursing home abuse is hardly a fairy tale. Most of it usually occurs on dementia units and it is often caused by another resident. Not always. Sometimes frustrated care givers with poor training may be responsible.

Be aware that libidos don't die or go away. Notice while you are there if your mom has developed a close relationship with someone.

Are they holding hands...eating together? Question staff about how the closeness of this relationship. Different people have different ideas about these issues. Some people are appalled if two residents with dementia decide to have a physical relationship. Others think it's ok. Remember both family members must be in agreement.

Dementia has nothing to do with intelligence and if two people want to be together in this way they will find a way to make it happen. Ask questions. Assist mom to the bathroom and see if you can find any evidence that this sort of activity has been going on. If you suspect it, report it.

If you suspect that the linen is not being changed you can make a small ink mark on the sheets or pillow case and check to see how long this sheet stayed on the bed. Some family members do the same thing with clothing or briefs. It is your family member's right to be clean and well groomed.

I worked in long term care a very long time. Most of the people I worked with and for are people who are truly committed to patient care. A few are not. Take the time to get to know the caregivers, especially the ones assigned to your family member. Remember that these assignments may change frequently and are often very different on weekends and holidays. If you have the time, get involved in the facility functions, such as family night or family counsel. Try to attend care plan meetings which are held every 90 days and as needed, even if it's only over the phone. That's a great time to get to know the social worker, dietician, and the therapist.   It is a state mandate that each resident have the least amount of chemical restraint that is effective. That means that meds that are psychoactive are frequently reviewed. You should always be aware of these changes, whether increased or decreased. Make it a point to be sure you are aware of all meds and you have signed consents for the psychoactive ones. If your family member has dementia, the most common will be Aricept, or donezepril. These meds do not cure dementia but have been known to slow the progression. These are not considered psychoactive but they can have some side effects of which you can be aware. Speak to the charge nurses to get a list of current medications. If you have questions about them, call the physician.

Be aware that physicians frequently do not round in nursing homes any more often than once a month. If your family member becomes ill he will need to go the Doctor. Sometimes the facility will make these arrangements, but you may be called upon to do the transportation. Even if they do the transporting they usually cannot stay with the patient during the visit. Be sure to make these arrangements before you admit your family member. Some people, like those who need very close monitoring or toileting care, cannot stay at the doctor by themselves. Frequently Doctors' offices will not transfer a patient from a wheelchair to the exam table. Be sure you speak to the doctor to see what those requirements will be.

People fall. It's just a fact of life in nursing homes. Falls can be caused by many different things. Sometimes a fall is fairly simple and requires no intervention. Serious injury and occasionally death may result in other instances. When a patient falls you and the doctor are to be notified immediately. This is the law. The time and date of the call must be documented. Also the reason, any injuries, the cause of the fall (if known) and any interventions that are put into place to prevent future falls.

Sometimes the cause is pretty simple. The patient slid on the floor. This is pretty common. Say for instance Dad usually gets up and goes to the bathroom by himself. But this particular night his blanket was on the floor and he slid on the blanket. Or maybe he was wearing socks and slid in the bathroom. (This is why those little socks you get in the hospital have grips on them). If there was no injury chances are you will get a call that says, "We returned him to bed straightened his blanket and called the physician. We saw no signs of injury we will continue to check on him every two hours for three days."

This information is documented in an "Incident Report" or an "Untoward Occurrence Report" and is the property of the facility. You can ask that it be read to you but it is typically not available to hand to you. In order to actually have it in your possession may require a court order.

Interventions that are pretty common with falls are:

1.   Floor mat alongside bed. (If this happens be sure floor mat is secured to floor. Otherwise it can cause it's own falling hazard).

2.   Call light within reach of resident. (this should happen anyway but they can get knocked down or pushed aside).

3.   Bed in low position. (This is used frequently in very confused patients)

4.   Bed/chair alarms. (some facilities don't use these as by the time the alarm sounds the resident has already fallen. Also they are easily disengaged during regular use).

You may be surprised to not see side rails on this list. Side rails have been greatly discouraged and for the most part discontinued in long term care facilities because of the danger they cause. It has been proven that confused patients frequently try to climb over them and have sometimes suffered serious injuries and deaths have resulted. Half side rails may be used if the order plainly states "To assist with positioning" but these also are being discouraged. Poles are being used instead of side rails for this purpose.

When I first started in nursing homes residents were restrained with Posey Vests, a kind of vest that was wrapped around a patient and tied in the back of the chair or around side rails. These are no longer used for obvious reasons. Now the state says the patient "has the right to fall" and a frequent faller must be care planned as such and interventions and outcomes must be reviewed with each subsequent fall. If the intervention was not successful then a new one must be put into place.

Yes there is a lot of documentation with long term care patients and with dementia patients it just increases due to need for extra care, psychoactive meds and behavior issues. It is your right to ask to see these care plans and definitely to participate in them. You will be asked to sign the care plan either in person or by proxy to verify that you are aware of interventions and agree to them.

There are also some medical reasons for falling. Some people (more commonly women) have osteoporosis and their bones can crumble. We used to think that people broke their hips when they fell. Now we know that sometimes the hip broke while walking and this caused the fall.

Dehydration, a common situation in long term care, can make a person weak, confused, and sometimes dizzy causing a loss of balance. Most facilities have hydration programs which are followed with varying success. Dementia patients frequently do not understand that they are thirsty. Other residents do not want to drink because they don't want to go the bathroom because they are afraid they will fall.

Urinary Tract Infections are also another cause of falls. They can cause confusion and pain.

Someone with dementia cannot always identify pain. Dehydration and UTI's seem to go hand in hand. It hurts to urinate so they don't want to drink. Sometimes in the elderly there are no obvious symptoms and new confusion may be the only tip off. In a patient with dementia this can be very hard to pin point!

Falls can of course often be related to medications. If a new medication is started and falls begin it is would pay to investigate the relationship. Not just psychoactive meds which can cause weakness, dizziness, drowsiness and confusion but also other medications such as blood pressure meds, heart meds, medications for diabetes and also some eye drops, such as timolol used for glaucoma have been known to lower the pulse and cause lowered blood pressure. Diuretics such as Lasix increase the need to urinate and may cause falls as a patient tries to quickly get to the bathroom. Pain medication, antianxiety meds and sleep meds, including over the counter medications can also increase risk for falls. Diphenhydramine, which is found in nearly all over the counter sleep medications, has been named as being dangerous for folks over 50. Be aware, be informed, be involved.

 If a patient tends to wander they may be placed in a locked unit with other people with similar issues. This is generally very hard on a family as guilt sets in. Seeing your Mom wander up and down a hall aimlessly with other people who are also wandering aimlessly can be heartbreaking. As much as the staff may try to keep all the residents groomed and well dressed accidents may happen and behavior filters don't kick in. Minor disagreements that used to be settled quickly may no longer be settled that easily, as a patient verbally or physically lashes out at someone over a real or imagined slight.

CHAPTER FIVE
STAYING HOME

Another option is to keep the person in his own home. Most people work outside of the home so this means either hiring someone to care for him or quitting your job and staying at his home with him. In Jerry and Ginny's case Ginny managed to work it out with her employer to stay at home most days. Jerry's brother came over a few times a week to give Ginny a chance to go to the office or do the grocery shopping or maybe even catch a movie.

In Texas a caregiver usually costs about $40.00 a day which covers about four hours. Of course sometimes other arrangements can be made. A live-in caregiver who takes part of her salary for room and board for instance. Or members of the family who come and divide different days. In any scenario keeping someone at home with Alzheimer's can be expensive....not only monetarily but psychologically as well.

At first, care may be fairly easy. Someone to be there to be sure he doesn't escape out of the front door, be sure he goes to the toilet and help him make a few simple meals. Maybe take him for a walk down the street. As the disease progresses, the caregiver may have to give total incontinent care, prepare a special diet (for instance a blended or purred diet when swallowing becomes more difficult) and assist him to bathe. Most, but not all, Alzheimer's patients, retain the ability to walk independently for a long time throughout their illness which in itself becomes a challenge.

Suppose you would rather care for your loved one in your own home. This is challenging but it can certainly be done. It's more comfortable for your mom (or dad) to be in a home the know, or at least with people they love and are comfortable with. As the disease progresses, it will certainly be easier for them when they are in familiar surroundings. There will of course be adjustments for everyone.
I strongly recommend that you find a good home health agency. Home

Health may provide someone to assist in bathing, skin care and occasionally assist with a meal. A licensed nurse will usually visit once a week to work with you on medications and instruct you in care.

Before embarking on the venture be sure to discuss with all family members, including children. You can say something like "Nana is no longer able to take care of herself so she will be staying with us. You can all help us to take care of her just as she has taken care of us all of these years."

You can get the children involved in helping to clear out a room, choosing simple decorations or pictures or even planning meals. You will probably want to bring some things from her home, maybe even some furniture. If you can get the children to become involved the transition will be easier. If Nana is someone the children have been close to they may have a lot of questions.

"Why can't she take care of herself?" "How long will she live here?" "Where will she sleep?" or even..."Will she die soon?"

Answer these questions as honestly and as briefly as you can being sure to answer only the question asked. Children tend to ask only questions that they can handle. Too much information can confuse them and frighten them. As they get ready for more information they will ask.

A safe place to sleep is usually the first concern. People in larger houses have turned a living room into a bedroom. If there is not a bathroom close to this room a bedside commode can be used to decrease falls during the night. Carpet squares as flooring often are used as these decrease the risk of sliding but are easily replaced as they are soiled.

Of course the bedroom must be downstairs but if the kitchen is accessible it may be necessary to be sure the kitchen can be locked off at night preventing night time "cooking".

All of the doors and windows to the house must be securely locked. Some people use an alarm system. A locked box with a hidden (but easily accessible) key must be used for medications. Sharp objects or those that can easily break must be removed. Electrical outlets must be plugged or blocked. Does this sound like a day care? In many ways it is similar. Remember that by this stage mom has reverted pretty much to toddler stage when she may become bored, restless and curious. All Alzheimer's patients go through pretty much the same stages as stated above so if she's not there yet, she soon will be. Preparation is key. You might consider a security system. There are many types. One common one is a door alarm. The patient wears a bracelet, either on the wrist or ankle. When he approaches the door an alarm sounds. This system is frequently used in professional facilities. Sometimes the patient can learn to pull a sleeve down over the device to block the signal. Another patient I knew enjoyed the attention and the sound of the alarm and set it off on purpose. But for the most part they seem to be pretty effective for warning you when someone is near an unsafe area. You would need to know how to not only buy the device but to alter the door so the receiver can be placed. If you choose to go this route be sure you have all the doorways alarmed, maybe even the kitchen.

Although they are usually not used in a facility, many people do have a bed or chair alarm for use in the home. This works well if you are in the other room and will at least alert you when someone has fallen or is getting up at night. Some people use nursery monitors. Sometimes people have hospital beds at home. These can usually be obtained from home health or hospice agencies through the DME (Durable Medical Equipment) companies. If you choose home health or hospice, they can be very helpful in obtaining equipment such as wheelchairs, hospital beds, oxygen equipment, bed side commodes, etc.

Ok so let's say you brought Mom to your home. You have the downstairs bedroom all set up for her. There is even a bathroom right off of her room to make it easy for her to toilet. You have contacted a home health agency and the nurse has come in to assess exactly how often she will be able to come. As the care giver, the nurse will discuss her medications with you and review exactly what she takes, what it's for and how often to take it. She might bring a pill box with her. If not, you can easily pick one up at the local pharmacy.

Be sure it has the accurate amount of times on it. Some are for four times a day, some for only three or two or even just one time a day,

The nurse will set it up for you for one week and work with you until you are comfortable with it. She will also leave you a written schedule to follow. She may refer your mom to physical therapy to keep her limber, and maybe even occupational therapy to help her with her ADL's. (Activities of Daily Living, ie toileting, eating, grooming, etc.)

Sometimes an occupational therapist can prolong the active phase by rehearsing and working with the patient to reinforce ADL's thereby making your job easier. Sometimes. No promises.

She may also request a speech therapist. Speech therapy can sometimes help with short term memory loss and also help to evaluate for swallowing problems. Dementia patients will eventually lose the ability to swallow and sometimes the therapist can help with this. She can also make a recommendation as to diet texture.

Does Mom need her meat ground? Pureed? Does she need her liquids thickened? If so to what consistency?

This may sound complicated but soon it will become second nature to you. You are entering a whole new world now. It won't take you long to navigate it.

Another thing the nurse will do is see how much help mom needs bathing. She may ask her to demonstrate her ability by getting into and out of the tub or shower and ask her to turn on the shower water. If your mom is unable to safely turn on the shower or get into the tub but can wash her body once she is in there she will be a "standby assist" meaning just what it says. You will help her get into and out of the shower, hand her the cloth and soap and stay close. You will probably hand her the towel and maybe help her with buttons or zippers on her clothing. If she requires more help than that the nurse may request a home health aide. This is someone who will come out twice or three times a week to shower mom, get her dressed, do her hair, help her with her shoes and socks. She will probably walk her to the living room and sometimes help her to the dining room table for a meal. She usually will not have time to assist your mom to eat.

Home health aides are typically not in the home for any longer than 30 minutes or an hour which usually gives you just enough time enough to clean up the kitchen, watch a TV show, or send an email or two. They cannot be left alone with the patient while you run to the store.

If the home health aide sees a change in the patient, such as a skin breakdown, bruise or maybe a change in behavior, she reports that directly to the nurse. The nurse handles all medical problems. The home health aide cannot usually change a dressing (not even a band aide) or give medicine. Sometimes they take vital signs. Not always. Typically an RN comes out every two weeks to do a supervisory visit in which they ask you how you are doing with your home health aide.

So you know about her medicines, maybe someone is even coming out for her shower, you might have some therapists coming out. Good for you. Home health is a wonderful help for you. We will talk soon about how to choose the right agency and when it is time to call Hospice.

For now, you are set. You know which foods to feed her, how and why to be sure she has regular BM's and even a phone number for the agency if you have a problem or if you see mom is getting sick. The agency will contact the doctor for you. Although they cannot take her to the doctor or even go with you it's helpful to have someone to lean on.

Remember, dementia patients frequently cannot feel pain or discomfort. They may become grumpy or moody and it can be difficult to tell if this a symptom of the progression of the disease or if this a medical problem.

Remember what we said about dehydration and urinary tract infections? It will be important for you to be sure she has water available at all times but as the disease progresses you may have to remind her to drink it. I usually recommend a pitcher of water in the fridge to be emptied every day. Don't forget most people urinate every two hours so you may have to take her to the bathroom during those times. When you do that you will be the most reliable person to spot changes. Is the stumbling while you walk her new to her? Is it because of her new slippers, a sore on her foot or is she really becoming weaker? Good subjects to bring up with your nurse. Your nurse may take a urine sample and take it to the lab to rule out a UTI. She may inform the physical therapist about the change in walking, or obtain a therapist if she doesn't already have one.

Because your mom cannot usually tell you when she feels well keeping doctor's appointments and observing her carefully will be very important now. Many medications may cause constipation so the nurse will ask you when she had her last BM. Constipation in the elderly is actually a leading cause of hospitalizations and may lead to death. It's important to keep on top of this.

Feeling overwhelmed? Yes. And it doesn't get easier. As the disease progresses she will become increasingly dependent upon you. She may need a bedside commode and ultimately, pull ups or adult diapers. You (or your designee) will be responsible for keeping her clean. Because urinary tract infections are such a big problem ask your nurse or home health aide to teach you the best way to change an adult diaper. It is a little trickier than baby's diapers simply because the patient is so much bigger.

It is at this point that many families choose to place their loved one in a nursing home. Somehow the thought of changing mom's diapers is a bit repugnant. However, many people do it and if this is what you have decided hopefully you will have taken my advice and obtained a home health agency to help you.

CHAPTER SIX
Making decisions

There are some tough decisions to be made. Among these: Code or no code? Feeding tube or not feeding tube? I recommend making these decisions with your patient it they are still able to contribute. If not you will need to sit down with your family (siblings, children, spouse) and make some decisions if they haven't already been made. By law if your mom stops breathing the nurse must perform CPR and she must be transported to the hospital. On TV all you see of a code (when patient stops having heart beats and breathing) may be the doctors and nursing pushing on the chest and inserting a tube down the patient's throat. It is actually much uglier. People vomit, ribs are cracked, and other awful things may occur. She may be placed on a breathing machine. If you sign an "Out of Hospital DNR (Do not resuscitate) other decisions can be made. Discuss this with your home health nurse. Other decisions you can make are covered in document called a Medical Power of Attorney.

People with Alzheimer's dementia most typically die of pneumonia. Some of starvation or dehydration. As the memory fades people may lose the ability to sense hunger, to chew food or even swallow. They may not know they are thirsty or remember how to pour water from a pitcher. It is at this point

88

that some families choose to have a feeding tube placed.

Having a tube placed is a surgical procedure. An opening is made into the abdomen that goes directly into the stomach. The wound is cared for until it is healed with the tube in place. Formula is poured down the tube into the stomach. Usually this is done with means of a feeding pump which alarms if the bag should be changed or if there is a clog in the tube. Water is ordered to help with hydration and medication. Pills are crushed, mixed with water and also poured down the tube, followed by water. If the tube is not kept flushed the milk can clot in the tube which can become messy, time consuming and sometimes means the patient has to go back to the hospital to get a new tube. The tubes must be changed periodically due to wear and tear. Because they are in the stomach eventually they begin to rot due to stomach acid. When the pump is used it can be disconnected for two or three hours a day to allow for bathing. When the tube is running the bed must be elevated at a 45 degree angle so choking does not occur.

Whether or not to "tube" is a tough decision. Medical power of Attorney one or two people will be delegated as the decision makers. That is usually the caregiver but not always. A Medical Power of Attorney is different than just a Power of Attorney which gives someone the right to make financial decisions. A Power of Attorney requires a lawyer. A Medical Power of Attorney does not. You can download those forms directly off the internet and fill them out and modify them in any way you like. If you have Home Health they have a social worker who can help you with the decisions and filling out the forms.

CHAPTER SEVEN
CARE IN LATER STAGES

If and when your mom becomes bed bound you will have to watch out for pressure areas. These used to be called bedsores, then decubitus ulcers. Whatever you call them they can become very serious very quickly. Cross your legs for about five minutes. You see that red spot? If you press your finger on it will blanch. (turn white). It take about two hours for a pressure area to form on someone who is either very heavy or very bony. A reddened area that does not blanch when pressure is applied is a Stage One pressure area. It happened because there was no blood flow the area.

Left in that same position with continued pressure the skin may break. The area will look like an open blister and as a matter of fact blisters are indeed Stage two pressure ulcers.

Continued in that same manner with no relief from pressure the surrounding tissues and muscle can be affected. That is a stage III. Continue longer you may have bone involvement. This is a Stage four. How long it takes to develop to these different stages depends upon the person. I have seen them go from two to four in a week. Once they pass Stage Two they are very difficult to heal. Eventually the skin begins to rot and an odor forms. Pressure areas are much easier to prevent than to treat.

Generally turning someone every two hours to reduce pressure prevents the formation of these areas. Also good incontinent care helps. Appropriate hydration and nutrition are important. Sometimes they are painful, sometimes not. Specialized air mattresses are available but I am here to tell you nothing works as well as good nursing care.

At home this may be difficult to manage. This means someone has to get up and dry and turn her every two hours throughout the night. Sometimes family members take turns with this. Most usually not. It's kind of like the new puppy syndrome. At first everyone wants to take care of the puppy. After awhile it's up to mom.

At some point you may seem like you are failing. Maybe despite your best efforts she is not eating or drinking enough. When the nurse comes to weigh her you both notice she is losing weight. Maybe she fell and broke a hip and although she was in the hospital she never really regained her strength or previous ability. Maybe she has a terrible cough that simply won't get better no matter how much medicine you and the nurse are giving her. At some point you and the nurse will look at each other and know. It's time. Depending upon the decisions you have made it may be time to consider Hospice.

CHAPTER EIGHT
HOSPICE

I have heard family members say, "Hospice! Oh no! They will just give him morphine until he dies."
That's not what happens with an ethical hospice company. Hospice is a family decision made with the physician. The hospice nurse will come out and evaluate the patient. They will look at weight loss, meds, quality of life. Most typically they will send a home health aide every day to assist with grooming.

Hospice is very different home health care. There are several components.
1. The RN. Just as in Home Health, She will make the initial visit, do the

evaluation, decide what the patient's needs are. She will supervise the care of the LVN and home health aide.

2.   Also as in Home Health, a nurse will do the weekly visits.

3   Also as in Home Health, a Social worker who will help you review forms, and assist in any way they can for social service needs

3.   Chaplain. This is different than Home Health. A Chaplain will be available to offer spiritual advice and comfort. They will officiate at funeral sometimes if needed.

4.   Medical director. When you transfer to most hospices the medical director takes over medical care.

I have known people to survive longer because of Hospice. They are compassionate caregivers who have entered this field of nursing because they have a very special calling. Sometimes having the extra attention helps people to get better. If your hospice company decides to discontinue the care they will explain why. It could be that the reason the patient was on hospice is no longer a problem. Weight loss for instance. If the patient suddenly starts gaining weight and stabilizes the hospice care may be discontinued and you can go back to regular home health care. Hospice care is heavily regulated by the federal government just as home health care and nursing homes are. They have certain criteria they must meet and most companies meet with the medical director at least once a week to discuss each patient and what changes need to be made. It's a very complicated system and ethical companies follow it closely.

The rules will change. Palliative care is what hospice provides. It means end of life comfort without an eye to recovery. They are all about comfort. Some people think that Hospice means that infections are not treated. This is not true. Infections cause discomfort so they will be treated. If you decide to send your mom to the hospital they will usually stop services until she returns, then resume. It is important for you to sit down with the hospice company nurse and discuss these issues. You may want to have a meeting with the

Administrator, Director of Nursing and the RN. It is your right to do this. You might want to interview several different companies.

Typically the LVN comes out once a week. At the point at which the LVN calls the RN, who is the case manager which a change, the RN will come out to assess the situation.
At this point, the decision for "CC" may be made.

"CC" stands for Continuous Care and it is usually ordered when death is imminent. Not always. Sometimes it's just a symptom that must be monitored. At this point, there will be nurse at her bedside 24/7 usually in 12 hours shifts.

If/when death occurs, the RN will be notified and she will pronounce death.

I had hospice care for my mom and multiple patients in facilities where I have worked. I will tell you that they were an enormous comfort and help to my family and I. I strongly recommend that you consider Hospice when it is mentioned.

Ok, there you have it. A rather grim guide but a necessary one. No matter which path you choose it is not an easy one. No rose-colored petals. Who dreams of changing their parents' diapers when they get older? Who wants to think about their dads chasing elderly women around a dining table?

CHAPTER NINE

SURVIVAL TECHNIQUES

There is a syndrome called "caregiver's syndrome". It describes someone who is tired, poorly groomed and depressed. That may be you. Remember above all to take care of yourself. You are your loved one's pillar now. Caring for a parent with dementia is a whole lot more complicated than going to your dad's house to help with yard work or filling a med box once a week.

Don't forget you have a sense of humor. As nurses we have very many funny stories.

Here are some of my favorites:
I talked to my patient about her memory loss. It was beginning to bother her. I told her about Aricept and offered to call her Doctor and discuss it with him. I discussed the side effects, (drowsiness, increased risk for falls, etc,) and she understood. A week later I saw her again and asked how she was doing with her memory pill. She said, "I didn't take it." Surprised, I said, "Why not? I thought you wanted to try it out." She said, "My son brought it over and now I can't remember where I put it."

Another time I walked onto a memory unit.
There was an elderly man lying in a Geri chair (a kind of reclining wheelchair).
Just as I passed him he reached for his crotch and yelled "There it is!"

When I am working in a facility and I need a pick me up I walk to the dementia unit. There is almost something wonderful going on in there. Part of this reason is because the people who choose to work on dementia units do it because they love it. Partly it's because of the patients themselves. One day I walked in to go speak to the nurse and three ladies greeted me and said, "Oh how wonderful to see you again," and hugged me. When I walked past them again on my way out they grabbed me again and said the same thing. Boy did I feel appreciated!

Laughter is still the best medicine. Always. If you can get a smile or a laugh everyday do it. Don't feel guilty. It's your due.

If your loved one had a hobby this is a good time to restart it. Did she play the piano? Listen to a particular TV channel? Did he like to garden? These kinds of activities have been shown to trigger a brain response. (and you may actually enjoy kneeling next to your dad planting flowers.) Some people have even had brief times of lucidity. I once watched a patient who didn't recognize her

daughter sit at a piano and play
perfectly.

CHAPTER TEN
GOLDEN RULES:

1.   Don't ever argue with a dementia patient. You will never win and you both will be frustrated. The best thing you can do is accept whatever they are saying and change the subject. If it happens again, repeat process. And repeat. And repeat. And repeat.

2.   Never, ever! accuse your patient. We once found a half smoked cigarette in my mom's robe. It scared my sister and I to death. Not because of the possibility of damaging her lungs but the possibility of burning herself (or the house.) We knew that if we asked her she would lie or just not remember. We checked all of her pockets, the room

and the whole house quietly. We found her stash in the silverware drawer. My sister quietly disposed of it and never said a word. The incident not reoccur.

3.   Remember safety first, last and always. Remove throw rugs, keep the kitchen secure. Keep all medicines locked up, including over the counter items such as stool softeners and aspirin, both of which can be fatal if over-used.

4.   Take care of yourself. Find some time to go the hairdresser, the movies, the nail shop. Don't forget the rest of your family. Enlist their help as much as you can but remember, they will still be there when this episode of your life is

past. Praise them effusively for their help but don't insist upon their engagement. Try not to whine. Instead keep a diary or start a blog. Go online and find support groups. See if you can safely allow your loved one to go to a day care group.

5.   Don't be afraid to ask for help. Maybe your church group or book club has members that would be willing to come over for a while.

6.   Lastly, as grim as this thought is, remember...it's not forever. This too shall pass. Spiritual help is invaluable to some people. As you care for your loved one your children and family are learning the meaning of commitment.

Care for your loved one is a shining example of compassion.

CHAPTER ELEVEN.
YOU ARE NOT ALONE

Resources you may find helpful. (Or at least interesting)

1. The SLUMS test. Despite it's odd sounding name the St Louis University Medical Status is a valuable tool for determining dementia. You can download it from the internet, print it out and give your mom the test. You will need another blank piece of paper. Depending upon your situation sometimes you can tell what you are doing. One caregiver I knew told her Dad it was a quiz she found on the internet and needed help with. Either way, it will evaluate at

which level of dementia she is at. Given every six months it can determine progress (or lack of it).

2.   Alternative treatments.
Much has been said lately about the use of Cannabis, or a derivative, CBD oil, in the treatment of dementia. At the very least this treatment may keep your dad calm. CBD oil does not contain THC (the element of marijuana which causes the high) but it has been known to be helpful because CBD destroys the brain tissues which overgrows in the brain and "tangles" the brain tissue. Some family members like it because it may help with arthritis pain. CBD oil is legal in most states and it is usually available at vaping stores. Be wary of buying it

online. If you choose to do this, discuss it with your physician. Not everyone reacts the same way to anything and if there an untoward reaction (increase in agitation or paranoia for instance) it is helpful if the physician is aware.

3. Become active in the Alzheimer's Association. They frequently have seminars and support groups to help you. Sometimes they have very good ideas and families similar to yours pool their resources, concerns and possible interventions.

CHAPTER TWELVE

IN CONCLUSION

I hope this book has helped you in some way as you begin this very difficult journey. Remember, you are not alone. There are millions of other people around the world who are also on this path. Reach out to them. Use the resources, the agencies, anyone available. Share the fear, the frustration and yes....sometimes...every once in a while, the humor of navigating the murky waters.

I would love to hear from you. This book is available as an audible on Amazon.

This and other books I have written are also available at Amazon.com/Lori Trotter

You may contact me by email at Lorindfw@yahoo.com or visit me at Loritrotter.com

Made in the USA
Middletown, DE
29 October 2021